MANDELA

First paperback printing 2008
First published in North America in 2005 by the
National Geographic Society
1145 17th Street N.W.
Washington, D.C. 20036-4688

Copyright © 2005 Marshall Editions
A Marshall Edition
Conceived, edited, and designed by Marshall Editions
The Old Brewery, 6 Blundell Street, London N7 9BH, U.K.
www.quarto.com

Paperback ISBN: 978-1-4263-0173-5
Trade ISBN: 0-7922-3658-0
Library ISBN: 0-7922-3659-9
Library of Congress Cataloging-in-Publication Data available on request.

Originated in Hong Kong by Modern Age
Printed and bound in China by Midas Printing Limited

Design: Starfish
Cover design: Two Associates
Series editor: Miranda Smith
Picture research: Caroline Wood

For Marshall Editions:
Publisher: Richard Green
Commissioning editor: Claudia Martin
Art director: Ivo Marloh
Picture manager: Veneta Bullen
Production: Anna Pauletti

For the National Geographic Society:
Director of Design and Illustrations:
Bea Jackson
Project editor: Priyanka Lamichhane

Consultant: Professor James Barber is a member of the Centre of International Studies at Cambridge University, England, and a Fellow of the South African Institute of International Affairs.

Previous page: This picture shows Nelson Mandela at age 38, in 1956, when he was leader of the African National Congress (ANC).
Opposite: Nelson Mandela, wearing the beaded necklace of the Thembu clan, poses for a photograph while he is on the run in 1961.

MANDELA

THE REBEL WHO LED HIS NATION TO FREEDOM

ANN KRAMER

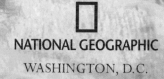

NATIONAL GEOGRAPHIC

WASHINGTON, D.C.

CONTENTS

EARLY YEARS

1

A SERIOUS STUDENT

2

IN PRISON

3

MR. PRESIDENT

4

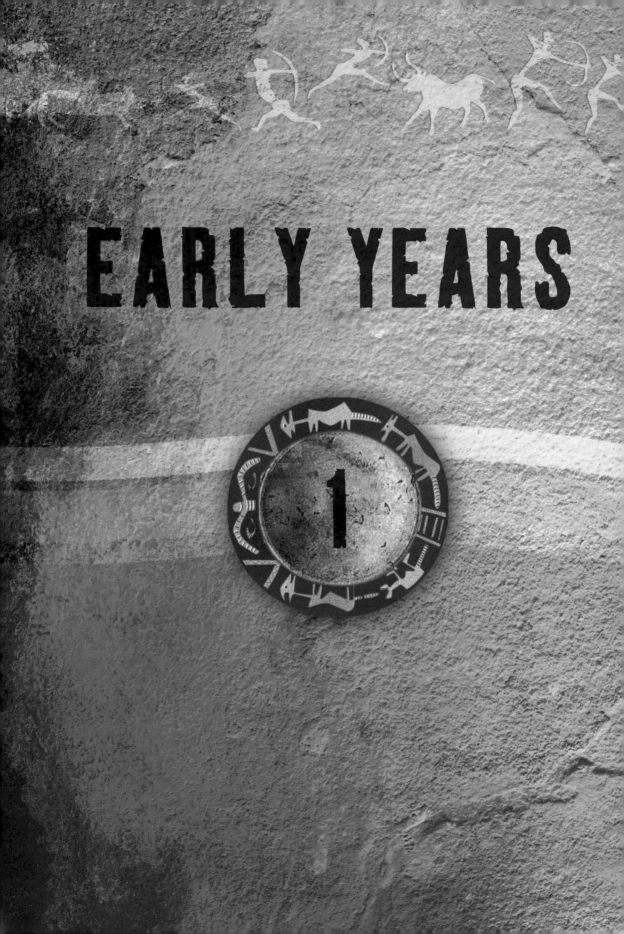

EARLY YEARS

1

Childhood on the Veldt

Nelson Mandela is the world's most famous South African. He led the struggle for equal rights in South Africa, spending 27 years in prison for his beliefs. In 1994, he became the first black president of South Africa.

Mandela was born on July 18, 1918, in Mvezo, a village on the banks of the Mbashe River in the Transkei region of South Africa. It is a beautiful area of rolling hills and valleys, with the Drakensberg Mountains in the distance. Mandela came from a large and noble family. They were Xhosa people, members of the Thembu tribe and Madiba clan. His grandfather had been a Thembu king. His father, Gadla Henry Mphakanyiswa, was a tall, imposing man. He could not read or write, but he was headman, an important person who settled village quarrels and advised the Thembu chiefs.

Left: Women did most of the physical labor in Qunu. They carried water, weeded, and harvested the crops. Mandela's mother grew all the food for her family.

Previous page: A Xhosa mother carries her baby on her back.

1910

The Union of South Africa is formed. White people, although a minority, hold all the power.

1912

The South African Native National Congress is formed to put forward black African interests.

Gadla had four wives and 13 children, and Mandela was his youngest son. He named him Rolihlahla. Mandela's mother was Nosekeni Nkedema, Gadla's third wife. She, Mandela, and her three daughters lived on their own *kraal* (homestead), where she kept cattle and grew crops.

Double meaning

Mandela's name, Rolihlahla, means "pulling the branch of a tree." It can also mean "troublemaker."

The local white people ruled the region and had the power to dismiss a headman if they chose. When Mandela was still a baby, his father quarreled with the white magistrate. There had been a dispute over ownership of cattle, and the magistrate ordered Gadla to appear before him. A proud man, Gadla defied the order and sent a message saying he would not go. The magistrate fired Gadla, who lost both his job and income. As a result, Mandela and his mother and sisters had to leave Mvezo to live with relatives in Qunu, a nearby village.

Mandela loved the country life. He later said his childhood years were among the happiest of his life.

Right: Mandela lived in a beehive-shaped hut. The walls were made of mud and the roof of grass. A central pole held up the roof.

1913
The Native Land Act is passed. Black South Africans are not allowed to lease or own land outside "native reserves."

1914
The white Afrikaner National Party is formed.

> *"From these days I date my love of the veldt, of open spaces, the simple beauties of nature."*
> **Nelson Mandela in his autobiography, *Long Walk to Freedom***

The village was larger than Mvezo, containing several hundred people. Cattle and sheep grazed on the village pastureland. Mandela's family in Qunu was poor, but he was now surrounded by loving aunts and cousins. Gadla visited them and the homes of his other wives in turn.

Mainly women and children lived in the village. Most men went away to work on large farms or in the mines. They returned twice a year to plow the fields. Women did the harvesting, weeding, and planting of crops. Everyone worked hard. By the age of five, Mandela was a herd boy, looking after sheep and cattle.

Daily diet

As a child in Qunu, Mandela ate corn cobs or maize (known as mealie), sorghum, beans, and pumpkins.

His mother looked after three huts. One was for cooking, one for sleeping, and one for storage. Mandela slept on the floor on a mat. During the day, he and his sisters sat on the ground as his mother cooked their food in an iron pot over an open fire. Smoke escaped through a hole in the roof. Mandela's mother grew all the vegetables and corn that the family ate.

July 18, 1918
Rolihlahla "Nelson" Mandela is born in the Transkei region of South Africa.

November 11, 1918
World War I ends. South Africa had fought on the Allied side with Britain and America.

As a child, Mandela wore blankets dyed with red ocher and went barefoot. In his free time, he played on the veldt with other village boys. He learned to use a slingshot to hit flying birds. He gathered wild honey and drank milk straight from the cow. He swam and fished. He learned to stick fight and rode bareback on calves. Other childhood games included hide and seek and *thinti*, a mock war game. Once, he fell off a donkey into a bush of thorns. He was embarrassed and felt humiliated in front of his friends. The Xhosa are proud people—Mandela never forgot his fall and always believed it was important not to humiliate others, even his enemies.

Mandela met few white people. The only whites in the village were the magistrate and the local shopkeeper. To the young Mandela, they seemed to be like gods because they had so much authority.

Left: Stick-fighting was a favorite game for young Xhosa boys. Mandela learned to avoid blows by moving away in one direction and striking in another, using quick movements and fast footwork.

1920
Mandela and his mother and sisters move to live in Qunu.

1920
Black gold miners go on strike for better conditions. The strike is brutally put down.

Xhosa: A Noble Background

The Xhosa are descended from Bantu-speaking peoples. They had moved about the continent before arriving in southern Africa around A.D. 200. Over time, the Xhosa divided into various sub-groups, including the Thembu. Every Xhosa belonged to a particular clan, or extended family. Mandela was a Xhosa from the Madiba clan. He was linked to the Thembu royal family through his great-grandfather, Ngubengcuka, who united the Thembu tribe and died in 1832. Mandela was descended from a minor branch of the royal family.

Over generations, the Xhosa extended their territory until it stretched along the eastern coast from the River Gamtoos to what is now Natal, and inland to the Drakensberg Mountains. They created communities, grew crops, and herded cattle. For the Xhosa, cattle represented wealth and social stability.

By the 17th century, Europeans were settling in South Africa. Beginning in 1779, the Xhosa resisted this European expansion. They fought a series of wars against the British and the Boers, who were originally from Holland. The British finally defeated the Xhosa in 1878. By the start of the 20th century, the Xhosa had been confined to the Transkei and Ciskei regions.

Left: Many Xhosa wear colorful necklaces, like this one, made of glass beads. More than six million Xhosa live in South Africa. A number have served as leaders of the African National Congress (ANC).

BOTSWANA
(BECHUANALAND)

TRANSVAAL

MOZAMBIQUE

• Pretoria

Johannesburg

Soweto

SWAZI-
LAND

NAMIBIA
(SOUTH WEST
AFRICA)

Sharpeville

ORANGE
FREE
STATE

NATAL

LESOTHO
(BASUTOLAND)

Brandfort

Durban

SOUTH AFRICA

Drakensberg Mountains

CAPE
COLONY

Transkei

Qunu
• Mvezo

Mqhekezweni•

Clarkebury •

ATLANTIC
OCEAN

Mbashe River

Healdtown•
Fort Hare•

Ciskei

INDIAN
OCEAN

Gamtoos River

Robben
Island

Cape Town

Cape of
Good Hope

Above: This map of Mandela's South Africa shows places
important in his life. They include Qunu, his childhood village,
Mqhekezweni, "the Great Place"; Clarkebury, Healdtown, and
Fort Hare, where he went to school; Johannesburg; and
Soweto. Mandela spent many years in prison on Robben
Island, which lies off the west coast near Cape Town.

Right: This beaded doll is Zulu. The Zulu are
linked to the Xhosa through similar origins.
In the early 1800s, they expanded westward
from their stronghold in the Natal region,
pushing the Xhosa out of Natal in a series of
wars and migrations known as the Mfecane.

Starting School

Few people in Qunu could read or write. Children learned by word of mouth and from the world around them. Custom, ritual, and tribal beliefs shaped their lives. When Mandela was seven years old, his father sent him to school. He was the first person in his family to attend.

Above: Mandela's first school, like this one, was run by missionaries. These Christians had come from Europe to "civilize" and convert Africans.

For the first seven years of his life Mandela learned from his parents or from watching life around him. His father told him about Xhosa history. His mother told him wonderful Xhosa legends that fascinated him. The young Mandela discovered there were many taboos (forbidden things) and strict rules. Like all Xhosa children, he was taught to honor his ancestors. In the small world of Qunu, boys followed the moral example of their fathers, and girls followed their mothers. Gadla was a father who demanded obedience.

A small number of Mfengu people lived in Qunu. The Mfengu had been attacked by the Zulu and had taken refuge among the Xhosa for safety.

1923
The African National Congress (ANC) is formed from the earlier South African Native National Congress.

1925
Mandela is sent to school in Qunu.

A European name

Mandela's first teacher, Miss Mdingane, named him Nelson. White people either could not or did not want to use African names, so all African children were given European names.

Unlike most Xhosa villagers, they were Christian; most of them had been educated in missionary schools. George and Ben Mbekela, Mfengu friends of Mandela's father, saw Mandela playing and noticed that he was smart. They suggested he be baptized and sent to school. No one in Mandela's family had ever gone to school. At that time, very few Africans did. Gadla decided that his son should go in order to better himself.

The day before Mandela started school, his father took him to one side and said he needed to be properly dressed. Up until then, Mandela had only worn a blanket over one shoulder pinned at the waist. Now his father gave him a pair of his own trousers. He cut them down at the knee and tied them with string at Mandela's waist. In his autobiography, *Long Walk to Freedom*, Mandela recalled, "I have never owned a suit that I was prouder to wear than my father's cut-off trousers."

Right: In Xhosa culture, boys like the one in this photograph listened to their fathers and did what they said. Mandela's father, Gadla, was strict. He taught Mandela about Xhosa customs and history.

1925
Afrikaans, the language of the white Afrikaner minority, is recognized as an official language of South Africa.

June 29, 1925
A bill is passed in the South African parliament to ban black people from doing skilled jobs in all industries.

Leaving Qunu

When Mandela was nine, his life changed completely.
His father died of a lung disease, and his mother could
no longer afford to keep him at school. He left Qunu
to live with a wealthy and powerful Thembu relative,
Chief Jongintaba Dalinyebo.

Mandela's father visited his wives regularly, usually staying
with each family for about a week each month. One night,
Mandela woke to hear a noise. He found Gadla, who
had arrived a few days earlier than expected, lying on the
floor of his mother's hut, coughing badly. Some days later,
Gadla died.

His father's death changed Mandela's life. He wrote in his
autobiography that he loved his mother dearly but his father
was his hero. Both father and son were stubborn and proud,
and they looked alike, with high cheekbones and narrow eyes.

1926
South Africa's autonomy is officially
recognized by the British government.
She remains part of the British Empire.

1927
Segregation (the separation of black
and white) is ordered in 26 urban
areas of South Africa.

> *"I felt like a sapling pulled root and branch from the earth and flung into the centre of a stream whose strong current I could not resist...a new world opened before me."*
>
> **Nelson Mandela in *Long Walk to Freedom***

Gadla had a tuft of white hair above his forehead. Mandela wanted one, too, and rubbed white ash into his hair.

Mandela's mother told him he would have to leave Qunu. He did not ask where he would be going. One morning, he packed the few things he owned and set out with his mother to walk to his new home.

Mandela and his mother walked westward for more than a day until they reached a village lying in a shallow valley surrounded by trees. In the center of the village was a large residence, grander than anything Mandela had seen before. There were two rectangular houses and seven *rondavels* (round thatched huts), all painted a dazzling white. A large herd of cattle and hundreds of sheep grazed nearby. This was Mqhekezweni, or "the Great Place," the royal residence of Chief Jongintaba, king of the Thembu people. As Mandela stood and gazed, Chief Jongintaba drew up in an enormous car. Tribal elders greeted him, shouting, "*Bayete a-a-a-, Jongintaba!*" ("Hail, Jongintaba!")

Family connections
Jongintaba offered to be Mandela's guardian because Gadla had helped him become chief of the Thembu people.

Left: Mandela tended flocks as a child, like this young shepherd gazing across to the majestic Drakensberg Mountains.

1927
Mandela's father, Gadla, dies.

1927
Mandela and his mother arrive in Mqhekezweni, "the Great Place."

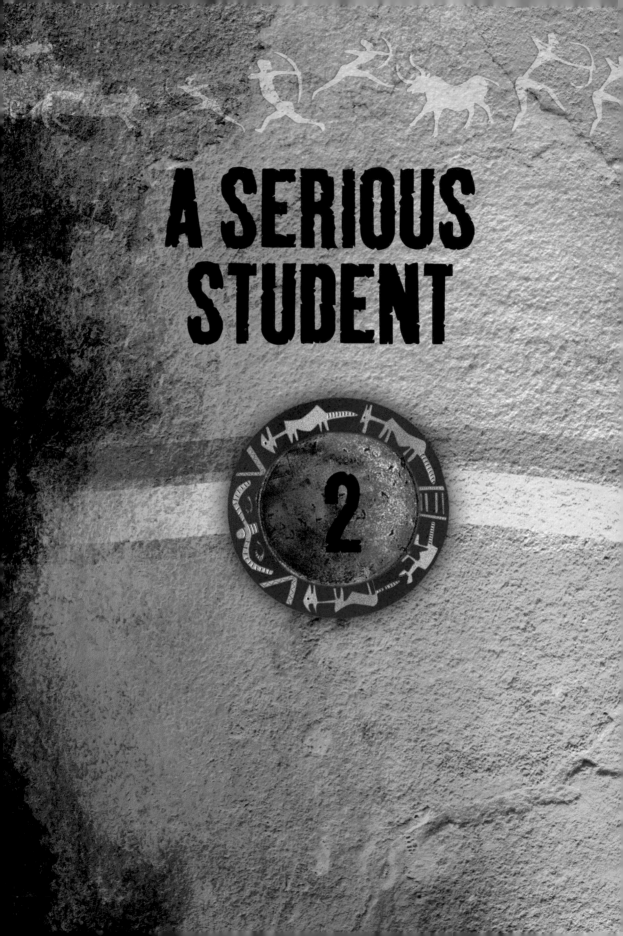

A SERIOUS STUDENT

2

Life in the Great Place

Mandela lived in Mqhekezweni for several years. Jongintaba became his guardian and treated Nelson as a son, raising him as an equal to his own son, Justice. For Mandela, life in the Great Place was exciting.

Mandela's mother knew her son would have a better life in the royal residence than in Qunu. She stayed a day or two in Mqhekezweni then returned home. Mandela was soon caught up in his new life.

Jongintaba and his wife No-England had two children: Justice, the eldest, their son and heir to the Great Place, and Nomafu, their daughter. The chief and his wife welcomed Nelson into their royal family. They raised him lovingly but strictly, treating him as if he were their own child.

For Nelson, the Great Place was a "magical kingdom." It was a missionary station and more Westernized than Qunu. Villagers wore modern Western clothes. The men dressed in suits. Women wore long skirts, high-necked blouses, and draped a blanket over their shoulder. They also wound scarves around their heads.

Nelson attended the local one-room missionary school next to the palace. There he took lessons in English, Xhosa, history, and geography.

Table manners
Mandela learned to use a knife and fork for the first time in the royal residence at the Great Place.

Previous page: Mandela is pictured at about the age of 21. He is wearing the first ever Western-style suit that he owned.

1927
Mandela arrives in the Great Place and becomes the ward of Chief Jongintaba Dalinyebo.

1927
The Immorality Act comes into force. Sexual relations between blacks and whites are forbidden.

The children wrote on black slates with chalk and read from *Chambers English Reader*. Mandela's teachers were Mr. Fadana and Mr. Giqwa. They took a special interest in Mandela and he did well at school. An aunt, Phathiwe, made sure he did his homework every night.

When Nelson was not at school, he had chores to do. He worked as a plowboy and herded sheep. He ironed the chief's suits and took particular pride in ironing the creases in his trousers. When he was not working or at school, he would ride horses, play slingshot, or stick-fight with other boys. Sometimes at night, Nelson and the other children danced, while young Thembu women sang and clapped.

Right: Mandela ran errands for the tribal elders. He fetched water and firewood, like this young boy, and told the women when the men needed drinks.

1928

The ANC organizes black workers in country areas of the Cape region.

1929

The League of African Rights is formed.

Left: There were regular tribal meetings at the Great Place, like the one shown here. All the male Thembu were welcome to attend. Jongintaba and his group of councilors listened to everyone carefully before deciding what needed to be done.

The Christian church had a big influence on Nelson. In Qunu, he had only been in church once, when he was baptized. Now he went to church every Sunday with Jongintaba and his wife. The local preacher, Reverend Matyolo, was an imposing man. To Mandela at the time, it seemed as if most African achievements had come about through missionary work.

Mandela was most impressed by great tribal meetings at the Great Place. White people controlled South Africa, but even under white rule, chiefs were important, and Jongintaba was highly respected. He played a major role in governing the region. He presided over the local tribal court and settled arguments. People came from all over Thembuland, bringing their problems with them to ask Chief Jongintaba and his council of elders to help settle disputes over cattle or land. Meetings often lasted well into the evening. A banquet was served, and Mandela sometimes gave himself a stomachache by eating too much.

1929
The white National Party wins the national elections in South Africa.

October 24, 1929
The New York Stock Exchange collapses, causing financial ruin for millions of people around the world.

Left: Moshoeshoe (1786–1870) was a great African king, a Sotho chief. He created the Basotho kingdom, now Lesotho, through clever diplomacy. Mandela learned about him in the Great Place.

Mandela watched the meetings carefully. He noticed that everyone who wanted to speak did so, no matter who they were. Chief Jongintaba and his elders listened carefully and respectfully to all. At the end of the day, when the sun was setting, Jongintaba finally spoke. He summed up what he had heard and tried to reach a decision that pleased everyone. If no agreement was reached, another meeting was arranged. For Mandela, this was true democracy. He believed it was a fair and just way to deal with arguments or conflict. He later said that what he saw at the Great Place influenced the development of his own style of leadership.

While at the Great Place, Nelson learned much about his history and culture. Elders told stories about Africa before the Europeans arrived, and of the Xhosa and Zulu heroes who had fought against the European settlers. The young Nelson listened quietly and was fired with enthusiasm.

Men only
Only men could speak at the tribal councils. Women were not allowed because they were considered second-class citizens.

1930
White women get the vote in South Africa.

December 1931
Black South Africans symbolically burn their passes in Durban. The army is brought in and violence erupts.

European Domination

The first Europeans to settle in South Africa arrived at the Cape of Good Hope in 1652. They were Dutch merchants and they founded a vital supply post for their ships on the Cape. But as more whites arrived they spread inland, seizing land from the Africans. They called themselves "Boers" (farmers) and later "Afrikaners," and they developed their own language, Afrikaans. In 1795, the British captured the Cape from the Dutch and formed a colony there, the Cape Colony. Unhappy with British rule, some Boers trekked inland, taking land from the Zulu, Xhosa, and Ndebele peoples. They created two Boer republics, the Orange Free State and the Transvaal.

In the late 1800s there were major discoveries of diamonds and gold—and both British and Boers wanted to profit from them. This led to terrible conflict. The British were the victors and took over the Boer republics, uniting the country as the Union of South Africa in 1910. The British government in London allowed the South African whites to rule themselves. Blacks formed the majority of the population, but they had few rights. Black people could not own land outside the crowded reserves allotted them, and black men needed a pass (written permission) to move about.

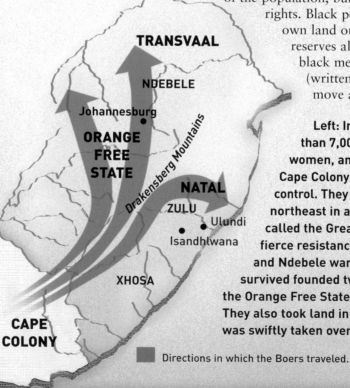

Left: In 1835–36, more than 7,000 Boer men, women, and children left the Cape Colony to escape British control. They migrated north and northeast in a series of journeys called the Great Trek. They met fierce resistance from Xhosa, Zulu, and Ndebele warriors. Those who survived founded two Boer republics: the Orange Free State and the Transvaal. They also took land in the Natal, but it was swiftly taken over by the British.

TRANSVAAL

NDEBELE

Johannesburg

ORANGE FREE STATE

Drakensberg Mountains

NATAL

ZULU

Ulundi

Isandhlwana

XHOSA

CAPE COLONY

■ Directions in which the Boers traveled.

Right: In 1879 the Zulus of the Natal rebelled against the British. They were skilled warriors. Under their leader, Cetshwayo, they defeated the British army at Isandhlwana. But the British brought in reinforcements and finally defeated the Zulus at Ulundi. The last Zulu rebellion was in 1906.

Above: The Boers, who believed they were God's chosen people, fought two bitter wars against the British. In 1880–81, they succeeded in keeping the Transvaal independent. However, in the second Anglo-Boer War (1899–1902), the British defeated the Boers, seizing the Orange Free State, Johannesburg, and the Transvaal.

Left: Many Africans, deprived of their land, were forced to work in white-owned mines. They lived in black-only barrack-style compounds. In 1920, 71,000 black gold miners went on strike for better conditions. Soldiers and police put down the strike brutally.

Becoming a Man

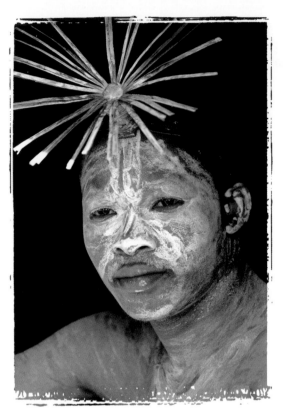

Above: Newly circumcised Xhosa young men are called *abakwetha*. An *amakhankatha*, or guardian, paints their bodies with white clay, the color of which symbolizes purity.

When Nelson reached the age of 16, he went through a traditional Xhosa ceremony to enter manhood. The ceremony was long and elaborate, and Mandela was proud to be taking part in the customs of his people.

In Xhosa tradition, boys must be circumcised to become men. An uncircumcised man cannot marry, inherit wealth, or take part in rituals. Jongintaba decided when his son, Justice, and Mandela were ready to go through the ceremony.

The boys, along with several others of a similar age, went to stay in two grass huts on the banks of the River Mbashe, in a place called Tyhalarha. The night before the ceremony, there was singing and dancing. The next day at dawn, the boys bathed in the river. Afterwards, they stood in a line, wearing only blankets. Jongintaba and other chiefs looked on while the ceremony took place. One by one, an *ingcibi*, or circumcision expert, cut off each boy's foreskin.

1933
The leader of the Nazi Party, Adolf Hitler, becomes chancellor of Germany.

1934
The South African Party joins with the Nationalist Party to form the "Fusion Government."

After the ceremony, Mandela and the other boys were painted from head to toe with white clay. Their guardian told them to bury their foreskins to symbolize burying their childhood.

Above: Before and after the ritual, the boys stayed in two grass huts away from the village. They told stories and prepared themselves for the duties of manhood.

The boys stayed in the huts until their wounds healed. When they emerged, they washed off the white clay in the river. The huts were burned and there were speeches, songs, and gifts. Mandela was given two male calves and four sheep. He had never owned anything before.

One speaker, Chief Meligqili, made a strong impression on Mandela. He spoke passionately about how Europeans had destroyed Xhosa culture. He said that the young boys had little to look forward to under white rulers. When Mandela was older, he said the speech had stirred something in him that influenced his political beliefs.

Act of manhood

To become men, Xhosa boys had to do a daring act. Once they would have fought battles or raided cattle; Mandela and his friends captured a pig and cooked and ate it.

1934
Mandela and Justice are circumcised.

1934
Mandela is sent to the Clarkebury Institute, a boarding school.

Boarding School

By the age of 16, Mandela's career seemed certain. Jongintaba wanted him to become an advisor to Thembu chiefs, like his father. He needed a good education, so his guardian sent him to boarding school and college. There Mandela learned British ideas and British culture.

Jongintaba sent Nelson to Clarkebury Institute, a missionary boarding school about 60 miles away. Jongintaba had himself been a pupil, and Justice was already there. The chief drove Nelson to the school and gave him a pair of boots, the first he had ever owned. He told Nelson to behave himself and never bring shame on his family.

The school consisted of more than 20 buildings, including dormitories, a library, and classrooms. Jongintaba introduced Nelson to the principal, Reverend Harris. It was the first time that Nelson had ever shaken hands with a white man. At first, Mandela found his new life overwhelming, but he soon adapted. One of his teachers, Gertrude Ntlabathi, was the first African woman to gain a Bachelor of Arts (B.A.), a university degree. Mandela studied English and history. He played tennis and soccer. All students had to do some physical work, so he worked in the reverend's garden. It gave him a lifelong love of gardening.

Meals at Healdtown

For breakfast and dinner there was dry bread and hot sugar water. For lunch came samp (coarsely ground maize), sour milk, and beans. The students ate meat three times a week.

1935
Anti-Jewish laws are introduced in Germany.

1936
Black voting rights are taken away in the Cape Colony.

Above: In South Africa white and black children had to go to separate schools. Schools for black children had far fewer resources.

When Mandela was 19, he went to Healdtown, the largest African school in southern Africa. There were more than 1,000 students, both male and female. Every day he got up at 6 a.m., had breakfast, and studied until 12:45. After lunch, classes continued until 5 p.m. After one hour's break for exercise and dinner, students worked until 9 p.m. Lights went out at 9:30.

Mandela took up new sports. Tall and thin, he seemed to be made for long-distance running, and loved running on his own. He also learned to box. In his second year, he was made a prefect, supervising other students.

1937

Mandela goes to Healdtown, a Wesleyan school in Fort Beaufort.

1938

Mandela finishes high school.

Running Away

In 1939, when he was 21, Mandela enrolled as a student at Fort Hare University. He did not finish his studies. Jongintaba arranged marriages for him and Justice. They did not want to get married, so they ran away.

Above: Fort Hare University College was founded in 1916. It was the main university in South Africa that accepted high-achieving black Africans. Many Fort Hare students went on to fight against oppression.

Mandela went to Fort Hare to study English, anthropology, politics, native administration, and law. He felt like a country boy, but soon began to fit in and make friends. One of his friends was Oliver Tambo, a science student and keen debater.

Mandela wanted to be a civil servant, an important career for a black African. He was a serious student, working hard at his studies. He joined the Students Christian Association and taught Bible classes at Sunday school in nearby villages. Sometimes on Sundays he went with friends to have a meal at a local restaurant. Black people were not allowed to eat in the dining room. Nelson and his friends had to go around the back to order what they wanted.

1939
Mandela attends Fort Hare University.

1939
World War II begins.

World War II had begun, and Mandela and his friends supported Britain. Jan Smuts, the South African Deputy Prime Minister, wanted South Africa to fight against Germany. When Smuts visited Fort Hare to speak, Mandela was impressed.

Above: Mandela (left) learned to box when he was at Healdtown, but he did not like to practice. When he was older, he took it up more seriously.

Mandela was elected to the Student's Committee but resigned in protest against poor food. The principal threatened to expel him. During the holidays, Chief Jongintaba announced that he had arranged marriages for Nelson and Justice. Nelson was shocked. He did not want to marry the chief's choice, but did not want to face his guardian's anger—so he and Justice ran away to Johannesburg. It was not easy to travel. After many attempts, a friend arranged a lift for them with a white woman. As black men, they had to travel in the back of the car.

Lack of freedom

In the 1940s, black Africans could not travel freely. They had to carry Native Passes at all times that showed they had permission from white officials to travel.

1939

The "Fusion Government" splits apart on whether to join World War II to fight against Germany.

1939

General Smuts wins the parliamentary vote and leads South Africa into war against Germany.

Johannesburg

Mandela arrived in Johannesburg without a job, money, or anywhere to live. His first thought was to find work in the mines. Later, he made friends and found a good job as an apprentice lawyer.

Above: In Johannesburg, black people lived in crowded shanty townships like Sophiatown, shown here, and Alexandra. Housing for white people was far better.

Previous page: Mandela is shown here in his 30s, while he was working with the African National Congress (ANC).

Justice and Nelson arrived in Johannesburg at dawn. It was a vast city, the largest in South Africa, and Mandela had never been in a city before. They went straight to the Crown Mines to find work. Both were given jobs— Nelson as a night watchman. But when it was discovered that they had left home without Chief Jongintaba's blessing, they lost their jobs.

Nelson went to stay with a cousin, Garlick Mbekeni, and decided to finish his degree by correspondence courses.

Mbekeni introduced him to Walter Sisulu, a businessman and black leader. Mandela's seriousness and royal connections impressed Sisulu. He found Mandela a job with a white law firm—Witkin, Sidelsky & Eidelman.

1940
Mandela and Justice arrive in Johannesburg without jobs or a place to stay.

1942
Chief Jongintaba dies.

It was rare for a black man to work for a white law firm. But this firm had black clients as well as white, which was very unusual. They liked Mandela and offered to article (apprentice) him free of charge. He was now 23 years old.

Mandela rented a room in Alexandra, a bustling and overcrowded area with unpaved streets. *Tsotsis* (gangsters) roamed the streets at night.

Above: Nelson Mandela was the only black student in the law department at Witwatersrand University.

But for Mandela it was all new and exciting. He worked as a clerk during the day and studied by candlelight at night. He also experienced racism and poverty in the city. His weekly salary was equal to about $4, hardly enough for the basics of life. Every day he walked six miles to and from work to save money. One of the lawyers, Sidelsky, gave him an old suit that he repaired constantly. It lasted him five years.

In 1942, Mandela passed his final exam and gained his B.A. degree. He enrolled at the city's Witwatersrand University to study law. It was one of only four universities in South Africa that admitted black students. There, Mandela was introduced to politics.

Empty cupboards

Mandela often went several days without food. His landlord gave him Sunday lunch.

1942	1942
Mandela completes his university degree through correspondence courses with the University of South Africa.	Mandela enrolls at Johannesburg's Witwatersrand University to study law.

Politics and Marriage

Many of Mandela's new friends were politically active. Mandela could see how badly black Africans were treated, and he, too, became a political activist. He also married and started a family. Protest in South Africa was growing, and it grew stronger still in 1948 when apartheid was introduced.

Life in South Africa was hard for black people. Most were poor and were often exploited by white people. They had few freedoms or opportunities. Mandela saw and experienced racial oppression. Many of Mandela's new friends, such as Gaur Radebe and Walter Sisulu, were politically active, as were his new white friends, who included Joe Slovo, Ruth First, and Nat Bregman. They wanted to challenge white oppression and improve conditions for black people.

Right: In 1943, 10,000 people marched to boycott buses in Alexandra after fares were raised. Mandela marched with them. The protest succeeded and the fares were lowered again.

1942
Mandela joins the African National Congress (ANC).

1944
Mandela marries Evelyn Mase, a nurse trainee.

Through Sisulu, Mandela joined the African National Congress (ANC), which campaigned against discrimination and fought to win rights for Africans. The ANC believed in peaceful co-operation. Mandela and his friends wanted action. So they decided to form an ANC Youth League in order to build up mass protest against white control. In 1944, the League was launched. Mandela was on the decision-making committee, his friend Tambo was secretary, and Sisulu was treasurer. They produced a manifesto calling for the liberation of Africans by Africans. In 1946, African mine workers went on strike. The authorities crushed the strike.

Above: Despite work and politics, Mandela spent as much time as he could with his oldest son, Thembi. He loved playing with him and reading him stories.

Mandela had met and fallen in love with Evelyn Mase, a nurse trainee. They married and rented a small house in Orlando West, later part of Soweto. Mandela and Evelyn's first child was born, a son called Madibe Thembekile (Thembi). Mandela was still an articled clerk, training to be a lawyer, so the family lived mainly on Evelyn's nurse's salary. In 1948, the white South African government introduced apartheid, a system that separated black from white and discriminated against the black population.

Few luxuries
Mandela's home had a tiny kitchen, a cement floor, and a tin roof. The toilet was a bucket. He lived there for many years.

1945 and 1947
Nelson and Evelyn's son Thembi (1945) is born. In 1947, they have a daughter, who dies while still a baby.

1948
The white National Party wins the elections, forms a government, and introduces apartheid.

Apartheid

In 1948, when the Afrikaner National Party came to power under Dr. Daniel Malan, Mandela was "stunned and dismayed." He knew that under the Nationalists conditions for blacks would deteriorate. Malan's government introduced apartheid ("apartness"). Laws were passed that formalized the separation of black from white. Black Africans were forbidden to go into white-only areas, they could not marry white people, and blacks and whites could not go to the same schools. In 1958, Hendrik Vervwoerd became prime minister. He made apartheid even stronger. His parliament passed a new law: the Promotion of Bantu Self-Government. Blacks were moved and resettled in so-called tribal homelands. Apartheid affected every part of the lives of black people. Africans, Indians (who had originally come from India for work), and some whites resisted, but protests were put down brutally. Apartheid continued until 1990.

Apartheid Laws

1949 Prohibition of mixed marriages: People of different racial groups were not allowed to marry.

1949 Immorality Act: It was illegal for people of different racial groups to have sexual relations.

1950 Population and Registration Act: South Africans were divided into four racial groups: "Coloreds" (people of mixed race), "Africans," "Indians," and "Whites."

1950 Group Areas Act: Different areas were set up in towns for different racial groups.

1953 Reservation of Separate Amenities Act: Blacks and whites were segregated, or kept apart, in all public places.

Left: White children play in a pond in the 1950s. The sign says the pond is for "European" (white) children only. Facilities for whites were much better than those for blacks.

Above: A white policeman checks a black South African's identity card. In 1956, passes were also introduced for black women. Some 20,000 marched in protest.

Above: A woman leaves a black-only restroom in the 1960s. Under apartheid, blacks and whites were not allowed to mix in public places.

Right: Black children play in a so-called Bantu reservation in North Transvaal. Under apartheid, black South Africans were moved into special black-only areas. Living conditions were usually dreadful.

Defiance and Treason

From 1948 onward, Mandela dedicated his life to the struggle against apartheid and organized mass protests against unjust apartheid laws. He was put on trial for treason. The police watched him constantly. His first marriage ended, and he met and married Winnie Mandela.

Above: Tambo (left) and Mandela set up their own law firm in 1952. It was the first black law firm in South Africa. Black clients flooded in.

Mandela and his friends believed they could force the white government to give black Africans rights. They did not want to use violence, so they called for strikes and boycotts. In 1950, Mandela became one of the leaders of the ANC. Two years later, the ANC, together with other organizations, launched the Defiance Campaign against apartheid laws. Mandela traveled the country calling for volunteers to break the law by going into white-only areas. The campaign lasted six months. Some 8,000 volunteers were arrested, including Mandela himself.

The apartheid laws remained, and the government introduced more severe measures. In 1952, the government put Mandela under a banning order.

1950 and 1954
Mandela and Evelyn's second son, Makgatho (1950), is born, followed by a daughter, Makaziwe (1954).

1952
Mandela and the ANC launch the Defiance Campaign. He is then put under a banning order.

Right: In 1958 Nelson met and married Winnie, pictured here. He and Evelyn had divorced the previous year.

He was not allowed to leave Johannesburg or attend meetings. He could not even go to his son's birthday party. In 1953, he was forced to resign as leader of the ANC or be imprisoned.

In 1954, the ANC sent out leaflets asking Africans how they wanted to be ruled. Thousands replied. The responses resulted in a Freedom Charter. It brought together all the organizations trying to make a free South Africa. Together they became known as the Congress Alliance.

In 1956, the government arrested many ANC and Congress leaders. Mandela and 155 other activists were charged with treason and with trying to overthrow the government with violence. The penalty for this was death. The Treason Trial lasted until 1961, when all of the accused were declared innocent.

Mandela and Evelyn had two sons, Thembi and Makgatho, and a daughter, Makaziwe. But their relationship had changed and the marriage had ended. Now Mandela met, fell in love with, and married Nomzamo Winifred (Winnie) Madikizela, a social worker.

Smart dresser

Mandela enjoyed curry and listening to jazz. More than 6 feet tall, he dressed in smart suits and drove an Oldsmobile.

1956–1961

The Treason Trial takes place. Mandela and 155 others are found not guilty.

1958

Mandela marries Winnie, a social worker.

On the Run

Protests against apartheid were growing. In 1960, the government declared a state of emergency, and the ANC was made illegal. Mandela went into hiding to continue the struggle in secret. He was on the run for 17 months, mainly in South Africa but also elsewhere in Africa and Europe.

Above: Mandela stands outside the Houses of Parliament, London, in 1962. Mandela spent ten days in London meeting leading politicians.

In 1960, South African police fired on unarmed protesters in Sharpeville, south of Johannesburg. They killed 69 Africans and wounded nearly 200, many as they were running away. The Sharpeville Massacre shocked the world. Mandela and his fellow activists organized a national strike and day of mourning. Countries worldwide and the United Nations condemned the South African government. Police arrested Mandela, Sisulu, and other leaders. The ANC was banned and Mandela spent five months in prison. When he was released, he was determined to continue the struggle, despite the dangers. In 1961, he left Winnie and their two baby daughters and went into hiding to organize protest.

1959 and 1960
Nelson and Winnie's daughters are born, Zenani (1959) and Zindzi (1960).

1960
The Sharpeville Massacre takes place. The ANC is banned.

Mandela knew he would be sent to prison if he was caught. He grew a beard and used disguises. He stayed on the move, traveling at night from one safe house to another. He had many narrow escapes, but he always got away.

Nelson met other ANC leaders in secret. He now felt that violence was the only way to defeat the government. It was decided the ANC would stay non-violent and Mandela would form another organization called Umkhonto we Sizwe ("Spear of the Nation"). They would carry out acts of sabotage against power stations and communications. Property, not people, would be the target.

Above: This picture of Mandela was taken while he was on the run. He is wearing a typical beaded necklace of the Thembu clan and traditional tribal dress.

Mandela and his colleagues hid out at Liliesleaf Farm, in Rivonia, a suburb of Johannesburg, while they planned armed struggle. In December 1961, Umkhonto carried out its first bombing. The government was taken completely by surprise.

Fictional hero
Mandela was nicknamed the "Black Pimpernel" after a man called the "Scarlet Pimpernel" in a novel by Baroness Orczy. The Scarlet Pimpernel was daring and bold. Like Mandela, he escaped capture.

Soon after, Mandela left South Africa for the first time. He traveled in Africa and Europe, raising support for the ANC. He saw how much freedom Africans enjoyed outside South Africa. On his return, he was arrested.

1961
Mandela goes underground. Bombings by his new organization, Umkhonto we Sizwe, begin.

1962
Mandela leaves South Africa and travels to Europe.

Life Imprisonment

In 1963 and 1964, Mandela and other members of Umkhonto were tried and sentenced to life imprisonment. They were sent to Robben Island, the harshest prison in South Africa. Mandela was 46 years old. It was to be 27 years before he would be freed.

Above: During the Rivonia Trial, supporters shouted "Ngawethu" ("We have the power") to demonstrate support for the defendants.

Mandela was charged with leaving the country illegally and was sent to prison for five years. While there, he was charged again—this time with sabotage. Police had raided Liliesleaf Farm and captured almost the entire leadership of Umkhonto, as well as taking papers and plans. Mandela and ten others were taken to court in Pretoria.

Their trial, known as the Rivonia Trial, lasted nearly six months.

Mandela knew there was no point in pleading not guilty, even though he could be sentenced to death. He decided to use the court as a showcase to explain his beliefs and how apartheid had forced him to turn to armed struggle. He took the stand in April 1964 and spoke for four hours. He said he had dedicated his life to the struggle for African people.

1962
Mandela is arrested for leaving the country and defying his ban.

1963–1964
The Rivonia Trial takes place. Mandela and seven others are sentenced to life imprisonment.

*"I have dedicated myself to this struggle for the African people...
I have cherished the ideal of a democratic and free society...
it is an ideal for which I am prepared to die."*

Mandela's closing words, Rivonia Trial, June 12, 1964

He explained that he believed in a democratic, free society. When he finished, the court was silent. The trial ended in June, and Mandela and his comrades were found guilty, but were sentenced to life imprisonment, not death.

Mandela and six of his comrades, including his old friend Sisulu, were sent to prison on Robben Island, where they were met by armed guards with dogs. Shouting orders, the guards put them into single cells in a specially built maximum-security unit—a prison within the prison.

Life on Robben Island was brutal. Even in prison there was discrimination—the prisoners were black; the guards were white. Prisoners had to wear short trousers, like young boys, and call the guards "bass" (boss). Mandela refused to do this. He and his comrades were category D prisoners, the lowest class, so at first they had the worst food and least privileges of all the prisoners.

Right: Robben Island is 8 miles off the coast of Cape Town. Originally a leper colony, it was a high-security prison. Escape was impossible because of strong sea currents.

1964
Mandela and six black comrades are sent to Robben Island. Their white colleague is sent to another prison.

1966
Mandela wins study privileges for the prisoners on Robben Island.

Above: This picture of Mandela (left) and
Sisulu (right) was the last official photograph
of Mandela before his release. It was taken
by a newspaper photographer.

Every morning, Mandela and his comrades were let out of their cells to break rocks in the prison yard. They were not allowed to speak. They had no clocks or watches. Mandela made a calendar on his cell wall.

After they had been in the prison a few months, they were sent to do hard labor in a limestone quarry on the island. The sun beat down as they used picks and shovels to dig out the lime.

Mandela and his comrades helped and supported each other. Mandela emerged as their leader, constantly fighting the system and demanding better food and conditions. Gradually, he won privileges.

The Rivonia prisoners were given study rights. They held classes and political discussions to keep the struggle alive. They nicknamed Robben Island "The University."

It was hard for Mandela to be cut off from his family. Visits and letters were rare, and he worried.

Keeping fit

Mandela exercised every day in his tiny cell. He ran in place for 45 minutes, did 100 push-ups, 200 sit-ups, and 50 knee bends.

September 1967
Malawi is the first black African state to establish diplomatic ties with South Africa.

July 1969
Thembi, Mandela's oldest son, is killed in a car crash. Mandela is not allowed to attend the funeral.

He heard that Winnie was being persecuted. She spent 17 months in prison herself. He did not get to see his five children for years at a time. But against the odds, Mandela and his comrades found ways of communicating with prisoners in lower-security parts of the prison in order to pass on messages and carry on the struggle in the outside world. They wrote tiny coded messages on toilet paper, hiding them in matchboxes with false bottoms, or taping them to toilet buckets.

In 1968, Mandela's mother died, and he was not allowed to go to her funeral. A year later his oldest son, Thembi, was killed in a car crash. Again, he was refused permission to attend the funeral. Mandela nearly despaired, but he was strong. He always believed one day he would be free.

In 1975, when Mandela was 57, he began to write his memoirs so the world would know about the anti-apartheid struggle. A released prisoner smuggled the memoirs out.

Right: Mandela repairs prison clothes on Robben Island. The authorities set up the photograph for English journalists to pretend that prisoners were not being ill-treated. Normally, Mandela would have been breaking rocks.

1975
Zenani and Zindzi visit Mandela, the first time he has seen his two youngest daughters for 12 years.

1975
Mandela begins to write his memoirs and they are smuggled out of prison.

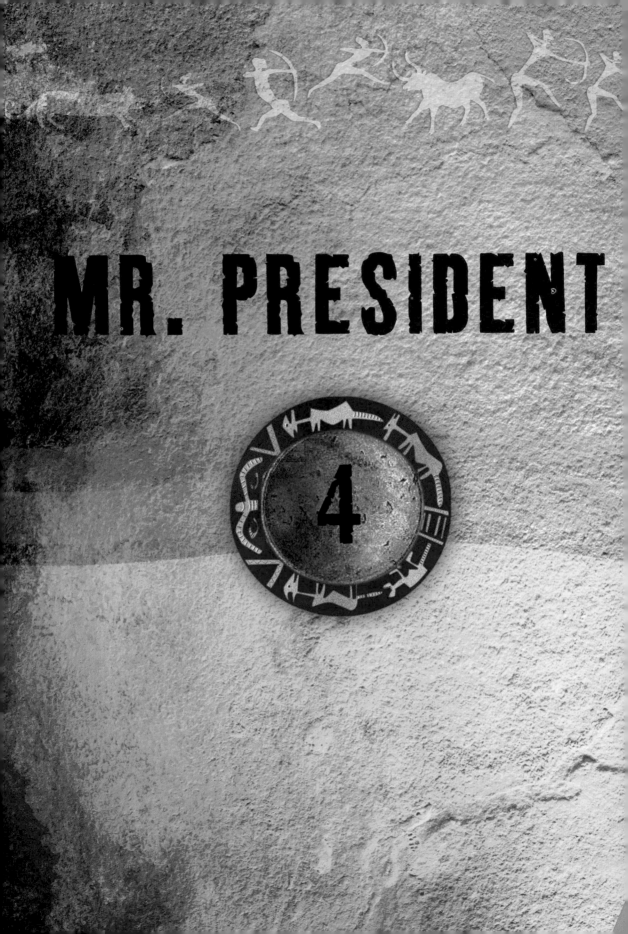

Free Mandela!

By the 1970s, conditions on Robben Island were improving. Outside prison, a new generation of South Africans was challenging apartheid. Mandela felt isolated from the struggle. But events would bring him to the forefront again. In 1980, the Free Mandela campaign began.

Inside prison, Mandela began to hear whispers about growing protests outside. Apartheid had seemed unstoppable, but in the 1970s, a new wave of protest began, particularly among the young. It was called Black Consciousness, and one of its leaders was Steve Biko. The government reacted harshly. In 1976, armed police killed more than one hundred protesting schoolchildren in Soweto. Black Consciousness activists were sent to Robben Island. Mandela was impressed by their bravery and called them "young lions." He recruited some of them into the still illegal ANC.

Prison conditions were finally changing. In 1975, Mandela and his comrades staged a work slow down in the quarry. In 1977, the Robben Island authorities ended hard labor.

Above: In 1976 a schoolboy protester is beaten and chased by police in a Cape Town township.

Previous page: Soon after his release, Mandela spoke at a rally in London, England.

1974
Successful liberation movements in Mozambique and Angola inspire black activists in South Africa.

1976
Black schoolchildren in Soweto protest against the use of Afrikaans at school. Police kill over a hundred of them.

By 1980, the political prisoners could listen to the radio and receive some newspapers. Mandela spent his time reading, preparing legal briefs for other prisoners, exercising, playing tennis, and gardening. He felt very alone—some of his friends had been released; some had died. In 1977, Winnie and Zindzi had been forcibly removed from their home and taken to Brandfort, a far-away township, so they could not visit.

Hope at last

In 1978, Zenani visited Mandela in prison with her husband and newborn daughter. Mandela named his granddaughter Ziziwe, meaning "hope."

Change was coming. In 1977, the police killed Steve Biko by beating and assaulting him. There were protests in South Africa and all around the world. Even white South Africans were beginning to criticize their government. Oliver Tambo, ANC president in exile, started a campaign to free Mandela. In 1980, on the anniversary of Sharpeville, Zindzi addressed white students at Witwatersrand University. She said that the release of her father was the only hope of avoiding mass bloodshed.

Right: Demonstrators outside the South African Embassy in London call for Mandela's release.

1977
The Black Consciousness activist Steve Biko dies in police custody.

1980
Umkhonto resumes a bombing campaign. The United Nations calls for Mandela's release.

Release from Prison

By 1982, Mandela was the main focus of protest against apartheid, and he was moved to Pollsmoor Prison on the mainland. Outside, tension and violence were growing. In 1990, Mandela was finally released from prison.

Conditions in Pollsmoor were better than on Robben Island. Mandela had a bed and a bathroom. He was allowed to hug Winnie for the first time in 21 years. In 1988, he was moved to a house inside Victor Verster prison.

The situation in South Africa was deteriorating. In 1981 and 1982, South African forces attacked ANC offices in Mozambique and Lesotho.

Below: Military tanks stand by while ANC supporters are buried. In the 1980s, violence surged in South Africa. The white government used increasingly brutal measures to stop protest. Many Africans died in the struggle.

1984
African Bishop Desmond Tutu receives the Nobel Peace Prize for his work against apartheid.

1985
U.S. Senator Edward Kennedy visits South Africa to show support for anti-apartheid protests.

Several people died and
Umkhonto launched further
bombings. Civilians were killed.

There was tension and
violence in the townships. In
1986, the government declared
a state of emergency. South
African president P.W. Botha
introduced changes, but
Africans, people of mixed
race, and Indians saw them
as an attempt to divide the
opposition. Despite bans,
anti-apartheid groups, trade

Above: Nelson Mandela and Winnie give the clenched-
fist ANC salute as they walk out of the gates of Victor
Verster prison to freedom in February 1990.
Thousands of people were waiting to greet them.
Mandela was 71 years old.

unions, churches, and students came together to protest in a movement
called the United Democratic Front.

Countries worldwide demanded Mandela's release and an end to
apartheid. More countries introduced sanctions. This meant that they
refused to buy South African goods or play sports with South African
teams. Botha offered to release Mandela if he would renounce violence,
but Mandela said he would not accept freedom if his people were not free.

In 1989, F.W. de Klerk became president. He released Sisulu and other
political prisoners. In February 1990, de Klerk lifted the ban on the ANC
and other anti-apartheid organizations. He announced in parliament that
the time for negotiation had arrived. A few days later, Mandela was freed.

1985
World-famous musicians release an
anti-apartheid record, *Sun City*.

February 11, 1990
President de Klerk removes the ban on
the ANC. Nelson Mandela is freed
after 27 years in prison.

Free Elections

Nelson Mandela was freed from prison in 1990. The then president, F.W. de Klerk, had accepted the principle of "power sharing." For the first time in South African history, whites would have to share power and government with Africans. Mandela and de Klerk met many times to discuss the form of a new multi-racial constitution. Progress was slow, and there were problems. Violence continued in the townships. There was bitter fighting between ANC supporters and Inkatha, a new Zulu political movement headed by Chief Buthelezi. Whites feared they would lose all political influence.

In 1993, Mandela and de Klerk agreed to a timetable for black majority rule. A constitution was introduced, giving equal rights to all South Africans. Between April 26 and 29, 1994, for the first time in South Africa's history, all ethnic groups voted in the first ever free democratic elections. Mandela was elected president, and the ANC won 252 of the 400 seats in the national assembly.

Above: Mandela gives the ANC clenched-fist salute. During the run-up to the election, he traveled all over South Africa campaigning for the ANC. Cheering crowds greeted him wherever he went.

Left: Mandela supporters show their strong feelings at an election rally.

Right: Nelson Mandela, ANC presidential candidate, casts his vote in South Africa's first democratic elections. He voted in a rural school in Natal, near where John Dube, founding president of the ANC, is buried. A journalist asked Mandela who he was voting for. Mandela joked that he had been "agonizing over that choice all morning."

MANDELA FOR PRESIDENT

ANC

Right and above: Lines of South Africans wait patiently to cast their votes. The election lasted four days. South Africa was more peaceful than it had been in years. For most black South Africans it was the first time they had ever voted; for many whites, the elections were a relief after a period of uncertainty.

1994 ELECTION RESULTS:
* ANC: 62.7% (12.2 million votes, mainly black—252 seats out of the 400-seat National Assembly)
* National Party: 20.4% (mainly white, mixed-race, and Indian voters)
* Inkatha: 10.5%
* Freedom Front: 2.2% (Afrikaner Nationalists)
* Democratic Party: 1.7%
* Pan-African Congress: 1.3%
* Other parties: 1.2%

Becoming President

In 1994, Mandela became South Africa's first black president. He was 75 years old. After years of struggle, the apartheid laws had ended and black South Africans had political freedom. But apartheid had divided and damaged the country. Mandela faced many challenges. His greatest wish was for unity, equality, and an end to poverty for his people.

Mandela said he wanted to build a "rainbow nation" in which all South Africans—black and white—would be free from discrimination. His first act as president was to form a government of national unity, by including the National Party. His deputies were Thabo Mbeki, son of an old friend, and ex-president de Klerk, an old enemy. Mandela had managed the transfer of power with little bloodshed, but the struggle was not over. He had to improve economic conditions for black South Africans. The gap between white and black was huge. Most black people lived in dire poverty, in poor housing without clean water.

Left: Mandela and his daughter Zenani attended Mandela's inauguration ceremony, May 10, 1994. More than 170 world heads of state were there.

1993
Mandela and de Klerk jointly receive the Nobel Peace Prize.

April 1994
More than 19 million people take part in South Africa's first free election.

Over the next five years, Mandela worked to ensure good relations with the white community. He encouraged white businesses to stay and invest in the country. He improved South Africa's image abroad. He met world leaders and invited

Above: Archbishop Desmond Tutu and Mandela greet one another. Tutu was awarded the Nobel Peace Prize in 1984, and headed the Truth and Reconciliation Commission.

them to see the new multi-racial, democratic South Africa.

Mandela introduced primary school meals and free healthcare for young children and pregnant mothers. But change was slow. There were strikes, increased crime, and outbreaks of violence. Mandela urged patience and an end to violence and looting.

In 1995, Mandela set up the Truth and Reconciliation Commission led by Archbishop Desmond Tutu, who had campaigned against apartheid. The commission investigated charges of abuse of human rights during the apartheid era. People were invited to give evidence without being prosecuted. More than 20,000 people told their stories.

Sadness

In 1996, Nelson and Winnie divorced. He had missed her dreadfully in prison but the marriage was now over. Winnie had fought for his release but was also involved in a murder.

May 10, 1994
Mandela becomes the first democratically elected president of South Africa.

1994
Mandela's autobiography, *Long Walk to Freedom*, which he had started in prison, is finally published.

Retirement

In 1999, at age 81, Mandela retired. He left politics, but for a while kept an active role in world affairs and his country. He remarried and went to live in Qunu, the much-loved village of his childhood.

Despite his many years in prison, Mandela had the energy of a man half his age. But early in his presidency, he decided he would not seek a second term. He told friends a younger man needed to take over. In 1999, the ANC won a landslide victory, and Mandela stepped down. Thabo Mbeki became president.

Above: Mandela and his third wife, Graca Machel, are surrounded by their family and friends singing "Happy Birthday" at his 80th birthday celebration.

A year earlier, just before his 80th birthday, Mandela had married Graca Machel, widow of the former Mozambique president. In 1999, they retired to Qunu, where Mandela had had a house built. Finally he could do the things he had missed during his long years in prison, in particular spending time with his family—his children, grandchildren, and great grandchildren.

1995
Mandela sets up the Truth and Reconciliation Commission, led by Archbishop Desmond Tutu.

1998
Mandela marries Graca Machel.

"*My hunger for the freedom of my own people became a hunger for the freedom of all people, black and white.*"
Nelson Mandela

Even during retirement, Mandela met world leaders, attended conferences, and received awards. He was democratic South Africa's greatest ambassador, welcomed and respected wherever he went. He did much to raise awareness of the AIDS/HIV epidemic sweeping through southern Africa. He also played a major role in peace negotiations in the Democratic Republic of Congo, Burundi, and other African countries. A lover of sports, Mandela secured South Africa's right to host the 2010 soccer World Cup. Mandela's legacy is remarkable. South Africa still faces serious problems, but the country is now a democracy in which every person—no matter what their color—has equal political rights.

Right: One of Mandela's favorite pastimes is to watch the sun set at Qunu while listening to music by Handel or Tchaikovsky.

1999
Mandela retires from the presidency and goes to live in Qunu.

2004
Nelson Mandela retires from public life.

Glossary

Afrikaans a simple form of Dutch language combined with African and Portuguese words. It is the language of the Afrikaners, descendants of South Africa's Dutch settlers.

ANC the African National Congress. The first and most important black organization in South Africa to fight for African rights.

apartheid Afrikaans word that means "separateness" or "apartness." Describes the laws that existed in South Africa from 1948 to 1990. Under apartheid, whites and non-whites were kept separate.

articled clerk someone who is learning the business in a law firm.

autobiography a book that someone writes about his or her own life.

autonomy independence, such as when a country rules itself.

banned under apartheid, a person who was banned was not allowed to meet with more than one person at a time or go to political meetings. Sometimes a banned person was not allowed to leave his or her home.

Boer Dutch word meaning "farmer." It was the name Dutch settlers in South Africa gave themselves.

boycott to stop buying from or dealing with an organization or a country as a protest.

clan a number of families who can trace their origins back to a common ancestor.

Colored in South Africa, a person of mixed race who belongs to a group that is not Asian, black, or white.

communist someone who believes in communism. Communists believe the state should own all property, and that people should work and be paid according to their abilities and needs.

constitution the written laws that govern the way an organization, such as a government, works.

correspondence course a means of studying for a degree from home, by receiving lessons through the mail and returning work to be graded.

custody the act of guarding. Someone who is in custody is being held under guard.

democracy a political system in which everyone has the right to vote, no matter what his or her race, class, sex, or religion.

elders wise men who know much about the traditions and customs of a tribe.

exile to banish someone from a country.

exploit the act of profiting from the labor of others without giving a fair return.

guardian a person who acts as a parent to a child.

hard labor compulsory physical work that a convicted criminal has to do.

identity card an official card containing personal details that people carry in certain countries, including South Africa.

liberation the freeing of people from oppression.

lime a white substance that can be obtained from limestone rock. It can be used to make cement for building.

looting the act of stealing, especially during a riot or disturbance.

magistrate a government official with the responsibility of making sure the law is upheld.

manifesto a public statement of the beliefs and intentions of a political party or group.

memoirs an autobiography, the written story of a person's life.

National Assembly the body that governs South Africa and makes the laws.

nationalist someone who works toward national independence. A nationalist may put national concerns ahead of wider, international issues.

ocher a reddish or yellow clay that can be used as a dye.

oppression the state of being kept down by cruel or unjust authority.

PAC the Pan-African Congress. A group of Africans who believe it is possible to unify the whole of Africa.

persecution the bad treatment of people who hold different views or have a different skin color.

privileges rights or benefits that, in the case of prisoners, can be granted or taken away.

racist a person who believes one race is better than another.

reservation land set apart for a special purpose. In South Africa, reservations were created to isolate and contain certain tribes.

ritual a religious or solemn ceremony.

sabotage the act of deliberately damaging something, for example a power station.

safe house a place that other people do not know about and in which someone can feel safe from detection.

sanctions the actions, such as withholding of supplies, taken by a person or country against another country to force them to change.

shanty a small, shabby home such as a hut.

sorghum a grass that grows an eatable grain.

state of emergency a situation, caused by political collapse or a natural disaster, that is officially recognized by a government.

strike the stopping of work by employees in protest against something, for example against the actions of a government.

township in South Africa, a part of a city that is set aside for mixed-race or black people to live in.

treason the betrayal of one's country.

tribal homelands the place of origin of a particular people, the land they come from.

veldt in South Africa, open grassy country with few bushes and trees.

ward a person, often a child, placed under the care of another.

Bibliography

Long Walk to Freedom, Mandela, Nelson, published by Little, Brown & Company, 1994

Mandela: An Illustrated Autobiography, Mandela, Nelson, published by Little, Brown & Company, 1994

Mandela's World, Barber, James, published by Ohio University Press, 2004

Nelson Mandela: Father of Freedom, Adi, Hakim, published by Wayland, 1988

Nelson Mandela: From Political Prisoner to President, Kramer, Ann, published by Franklin Watts, 2003

South Africa in the 20th Century, Barber, James, published by Blackwell Publishers, 1999

Sources of quotes:
p.10　*Long Walk to Freedom*, p.11
p.15　*Long Walk to Freedom*, p.15
p.17　*Long Walk to Freedom*, p.19
p.45　*Long Walk to Freedom*, p.438
p.59　*Long Walk to Freedom*, p.751

Some websites that will help you to explore the life and world of Nelson Mandela:
www.anc.org.za/people/mandela.html
www.pbs.org/wgbh/pages/frontline/shows/ mandela/
www.sahistory.org.za
www.southafrica-travel.net/history/ eh_menu.htm
www.time.com/time/time100/leaders/profile/ mandela.html

Index

Acknowledgments

B = bottom, C = center, T = top, L = left, R = right.

Front cover Rex Features/Sipa; **1C** Rex Features/Sipa; **1** Getty Images/Time Life Pictures; **1B** Rex Features/ Eddie Boldizsar; **3** Corbis/Herve Collart; **3C** Rex Features/Sipa; **4T** Getty Images/National Geographic; **4B** Rex Features/Sipa; **5T** Rex Features/Sipa; **5B** Corbis/© Peter Turnley; **7** Getty Images/National Geographic; **8** Corbis/© Bettmann; **9** Still Pictures/Hjalte Tin; **11** Corbis/© Roger De La Harpe, Gallo Images; **12** The Art Archive/Dagli Orti; **13** Werner Forman Archive/Anspach Collection, New York; **14** Getty Images/Hulton Archive; **15** Corbis/© Roger De La Harpe, Gallo Images; **16** Corbis/© Hulton-Deutsch Collection; **19** Rex Features/Sipa; **21** Corbis/© Bettmann; **22** South Photographs/Guy Tillim; **23** The Art Archive; **25TR** The Art Archive; **25C** Getty Images/Hulton Archive; **25B** L.P.Pictures; **26** Corbis/© Gallo Images; **27** Getty Images/Per-Anders Pettersson; **29** Getty Images/Time Life Pictures; **30** Topfoto/AP; **31** Bob Gosani © Baileys African History Archive; **33** Rex Features/Sipa; **34** Corbis/ © Bettmann; **35** Topfoto; **36** UWC-Robben Island Museum Mayibuye Archives; **37** UWC-Robben Island Museum Mayibuye Archives; **38** Getty Images/Hulton Archive; **39TL** Getty Images/Hulton Archive; **39TR** Corbis/© Bettmann; **39B** Getty Images/Hulton Archive; **40** Rex Features/Sipa; **41** Getty Images/ Hulton Archive; **42** Getty Images/Hulton Archive; **43** Rex Features/Sipa; **44** Topfoto/AP; **45** Corbis/© Gallo Images; **46** Getty Images/Hulton Archive; **47** Getty Images/Hulton Archive; **49** Corbis/© Peter Turnley; **50** Link/UWC-Robben Island Museum Mayibuye Archives; **51** Rex Features/Eddie Boldizsar; **52** Corbis/ © Gideon Mendel; **53** Corbis/© Reuters; **54–55** Corbis/© Peter Turnley; **54T** Getty Images/Time Life Pictures; **54B** Corbis/© Peter Turnley; **55B** Corbis/© Peter Turnley; **56** Corbis/© David Turnley; **57** Getty Images/AFP; **58** Corbis/Herbert Mabuza; **59** Corbis Saba/© Louise Gubb.